GRAPHIC LIBRARY

GRAPHIC SCIENCE

THE ATTRACTIVE STORY OF MAGNETISM

WITH MAX AXIOM SUPER SCIENTIST

by Andrea Gianopoulos | illustrated by Cynthia Martin and Barbara Schulz

Consultant:
Leslie Flynn, PhD
Science Education
University of Minnesota

CAPSTONE PRESS
a capstone imprint

Graphic Library is published by Capstone Press,
1710 Roe Crest Drive, North Mankato, Minnesota 56003.
www.mycapstone.com

Library of Congress Cataloging-in-Publication Data is available on the Library of Congress website.
ISBN: 978-1-5435-2950-0 (library binding)
ISBN: 978-1-5435-2961-6 (paperback)
ISBN: 978-1-5435-2971-5 (eBook PDF)

Summary: In graphic novel format, follows the adventures of Max Axiom as he explains the science behind magnetism.

Art Director and Designer
Bob Lentz

Colorist
Krista Ward

Cover Artist
Tod Smith

Editor
Christopher L. Harbo

Photo Credits
Capstone Studio/Karon Dubke: 29

Printed in the United States 6059

TABLE OF CONTENTS

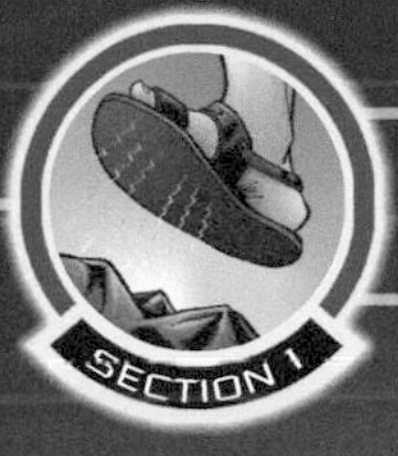
SECTION 1

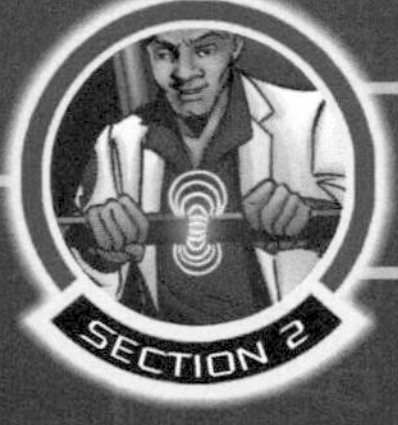
SECTION 2

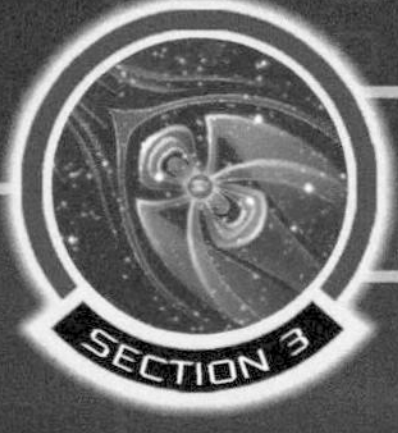
SECTION 3

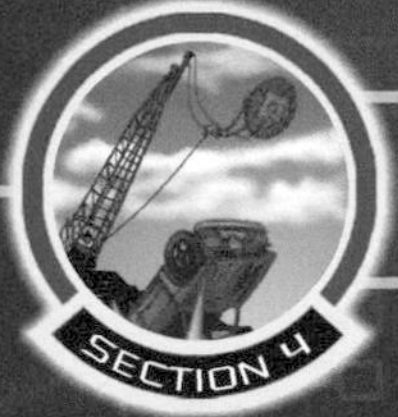
SECTION 4

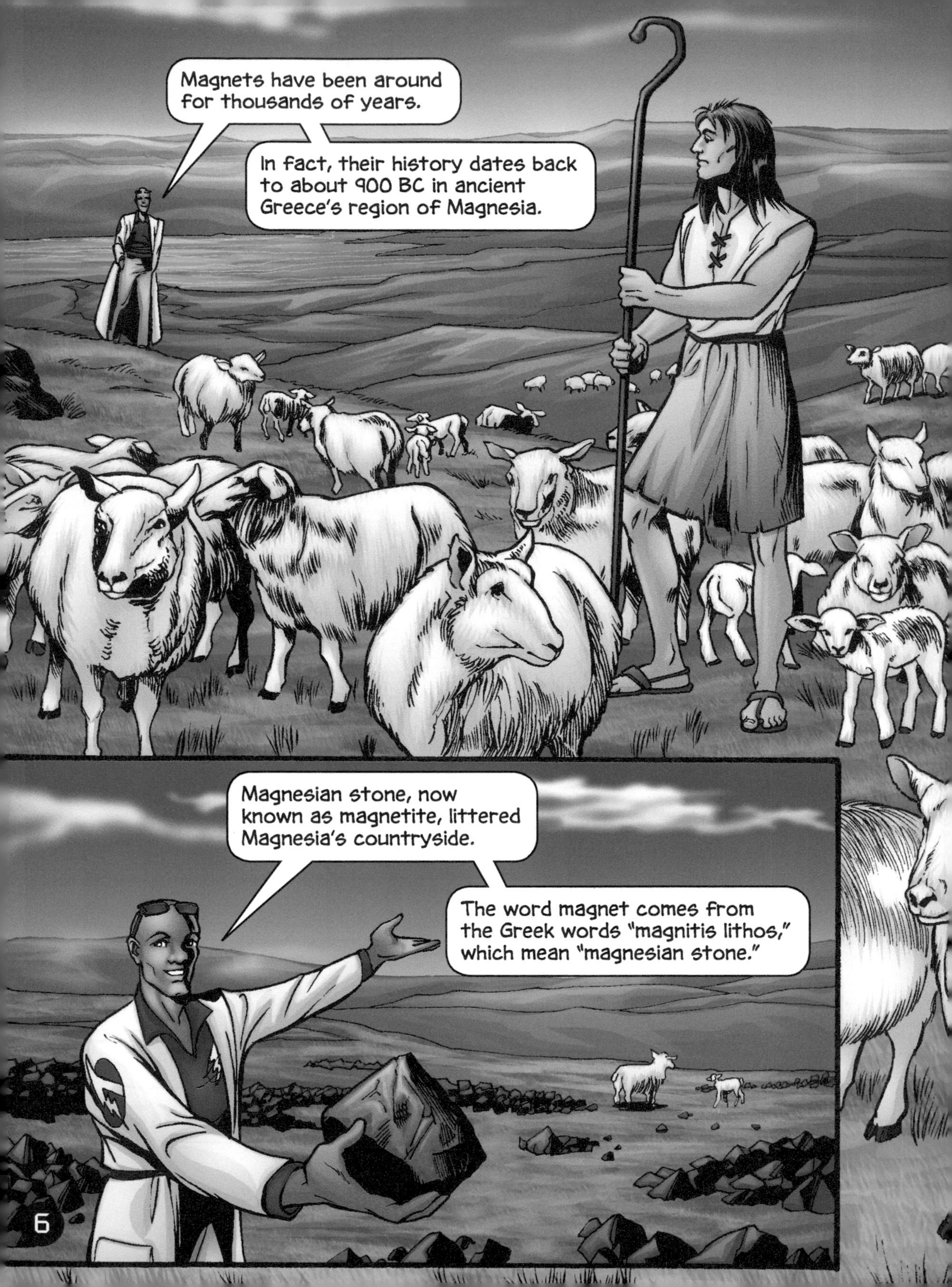

Magnets have been around for thousands of years.
In fact, their history dates back to about 900 BC in ancient Greece's region of Magnesia.
Magnesian stone, now known as magnetite, littered Magnesia's countryside.
The word magnet comes from the Greek words "magnitis lithos," which mean "magnesian stone."

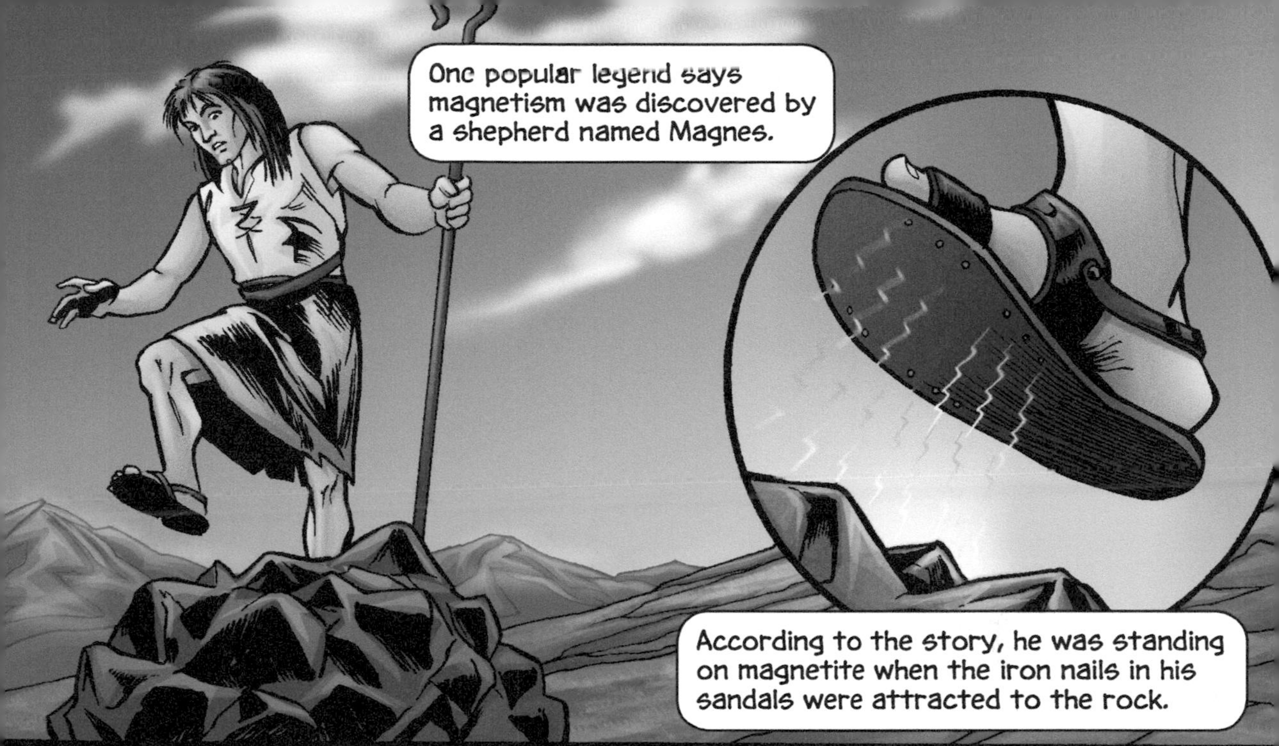
One popular legend says magnetism was discovered by a shepherd named Magnes.
According to the story, he was standing on magnetite when the iron nails in his sandals were attracted to the rock.

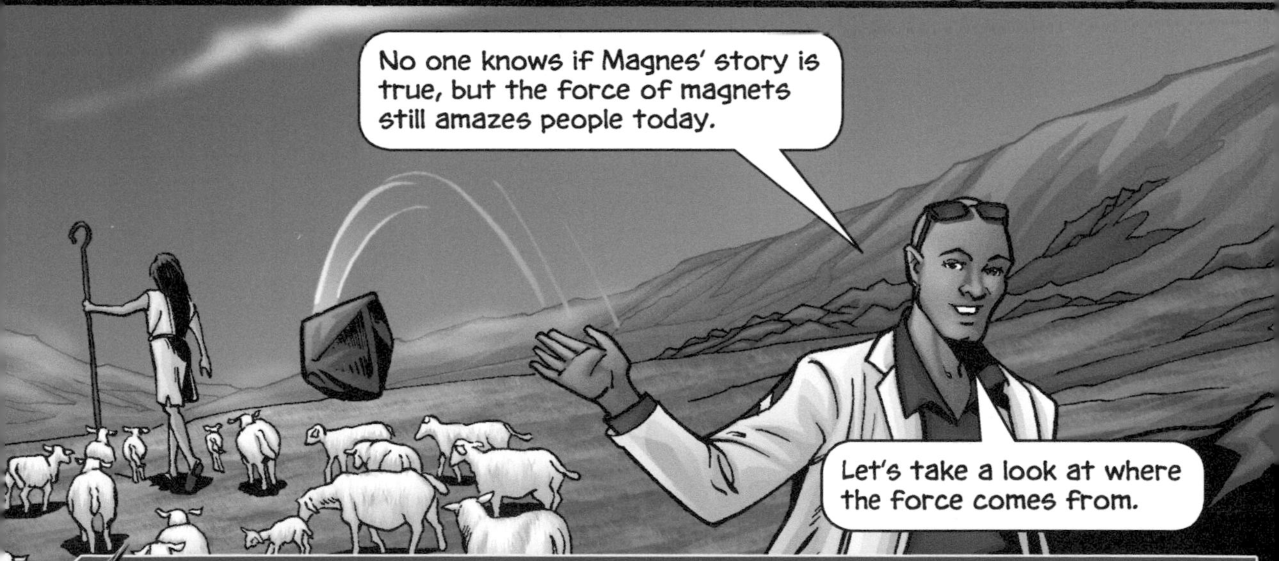
No one knows if Magnes' story is true, but the force of magnets still amazes people today.
Let's take a look at where the force comes from.

MAGNETIC MATERIALS

ACCESS GRANTED: MAX AXIOM

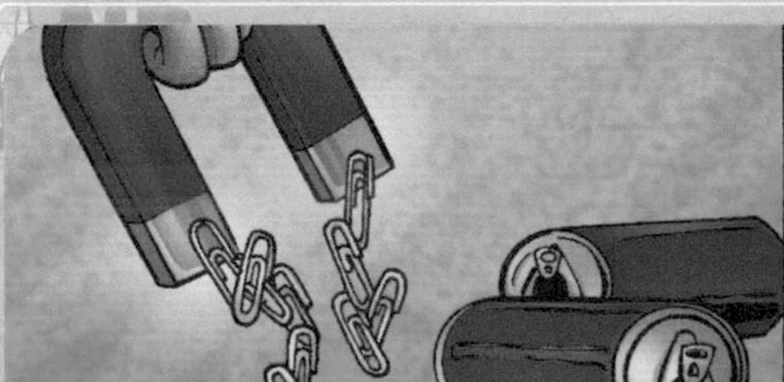

Magnetism attracts some metals, but not others. A magnet will easily pick up iron, steel, nickel, and cobalt. But it has no power over aluminum, copper, or gold.

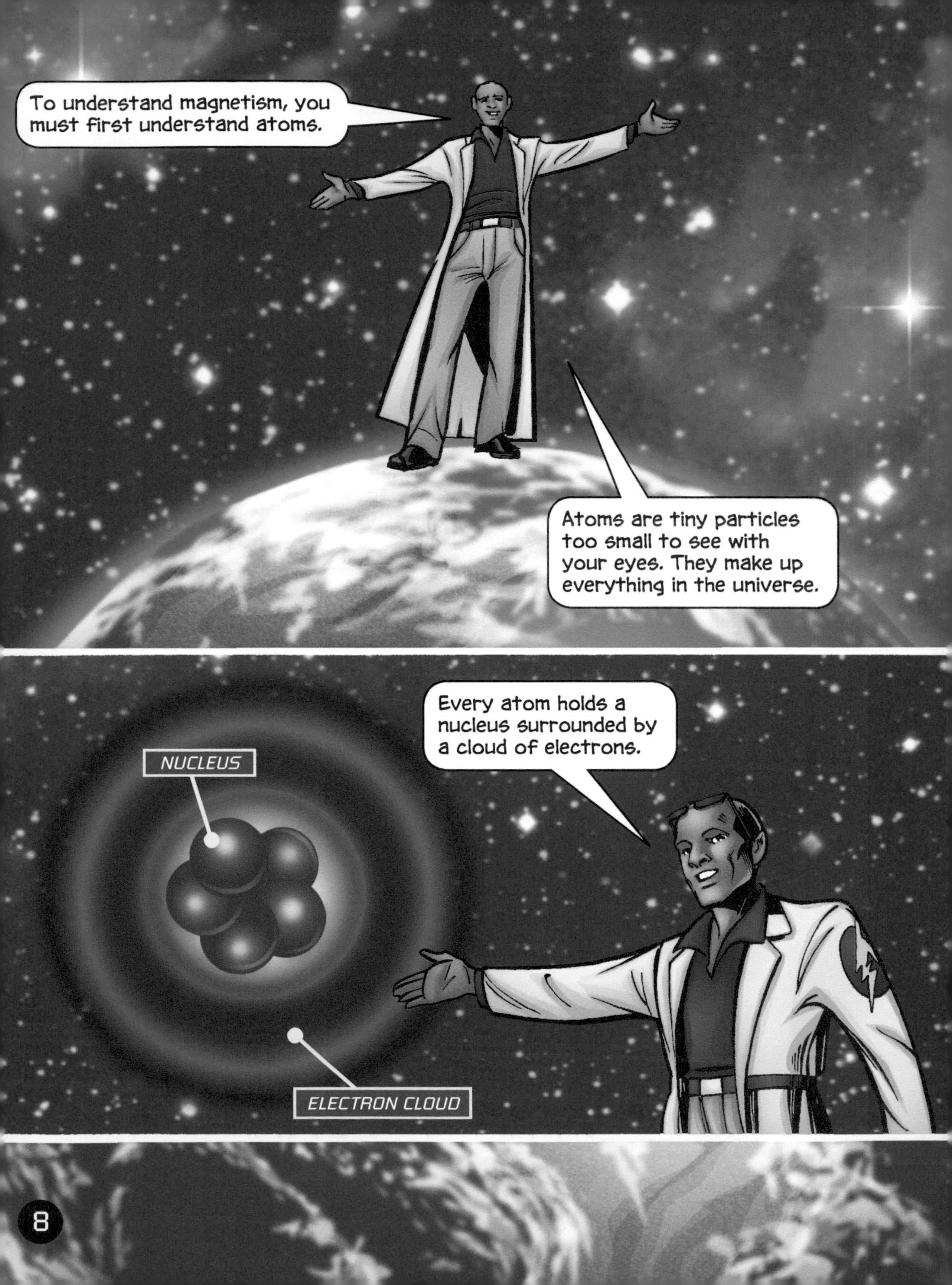
To understand magnetism, you must first understand atoms.
Atoms are tiny particles too small to see with your eyes. They make up everything in the universe.
Every atom holds a nucleus surrounded by a cloud of electrons.
NUCLEUS
ELECTRON CLOUD

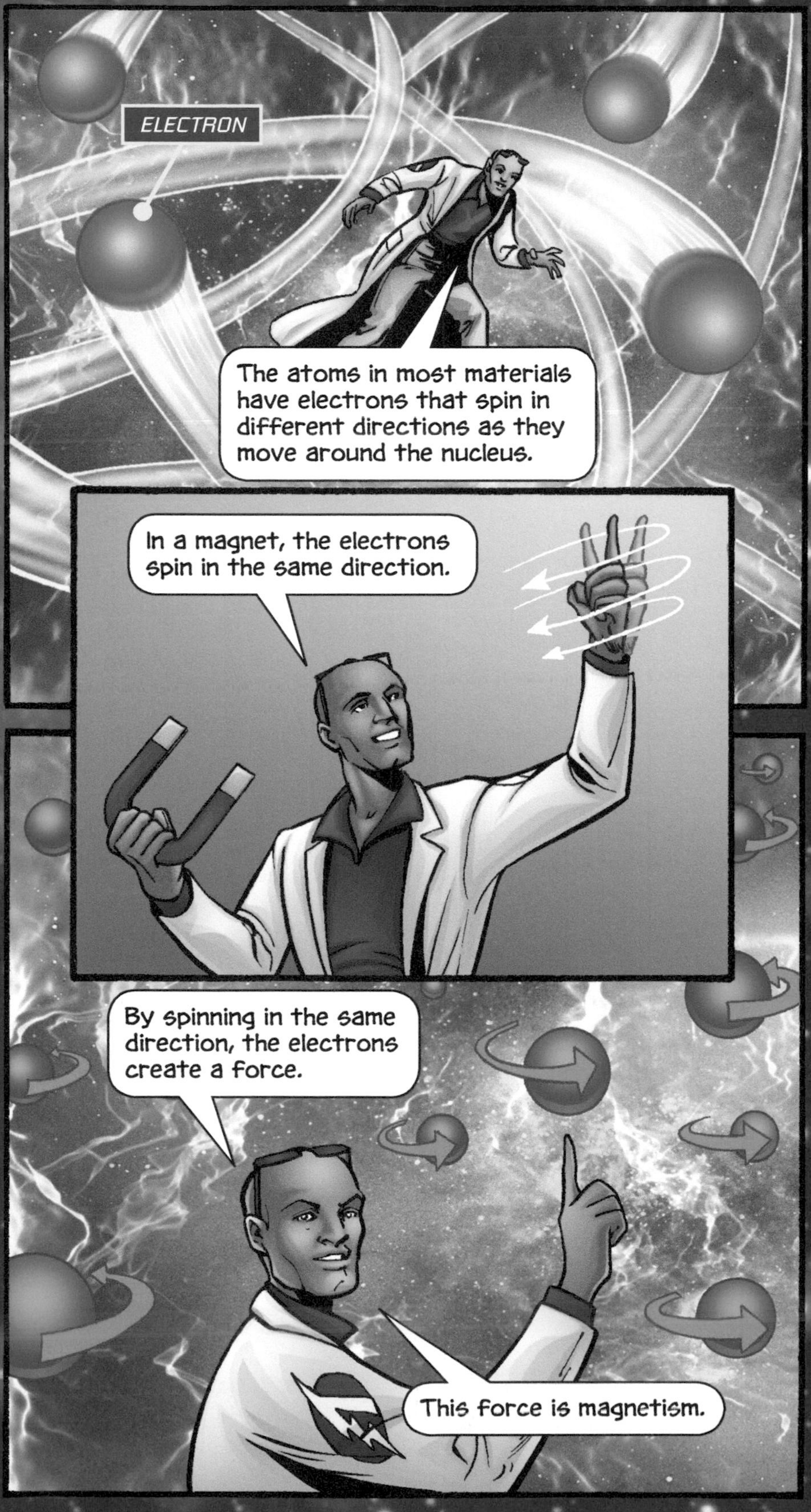
ELECTRON
The atoms in most materials have electrons that spin in different directions as they move around the nucleus.
In a magnet, the electrons spin in the same direction.
By spinning in the same direction, the electrons create a force.
This force is magnetism.

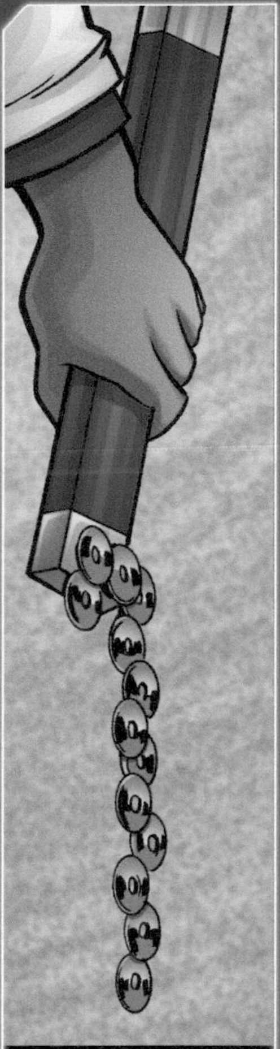

Magnets pass their magnetic power to the objects they attract. A steel washer stuck to a magnet becomes a temporary magnet itself. In fact, a chain of washers can dangle from the magnet as the magnetic force is passed from one washer to the next.

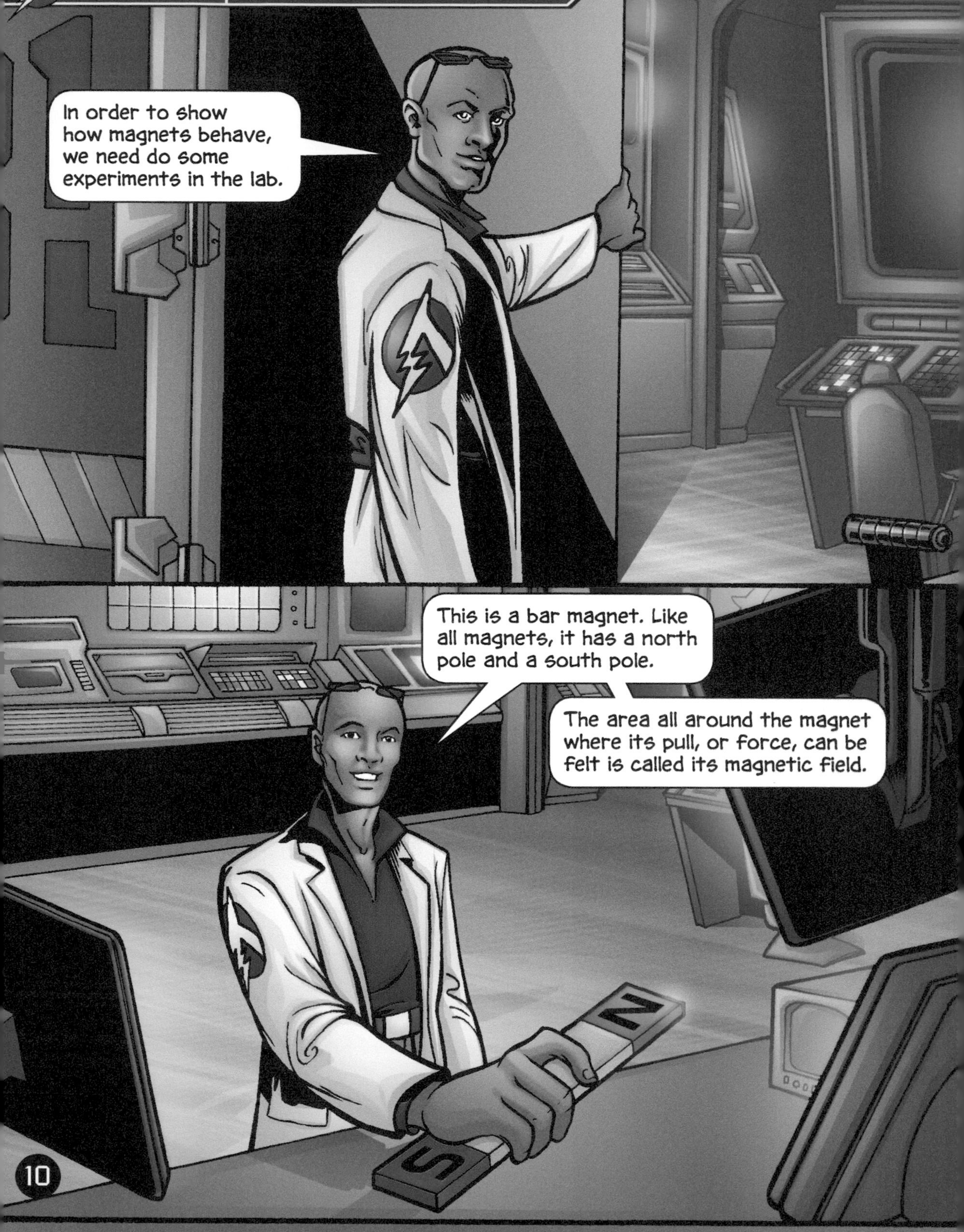
In order to show how magnets behave, we need do some experiments in the lab.
This is a bar magnet. Like all magnets, it has a north pole and a south pole.
The area all around the magnet where its pull, or force, can be felt is called its magnetic field.
N
S

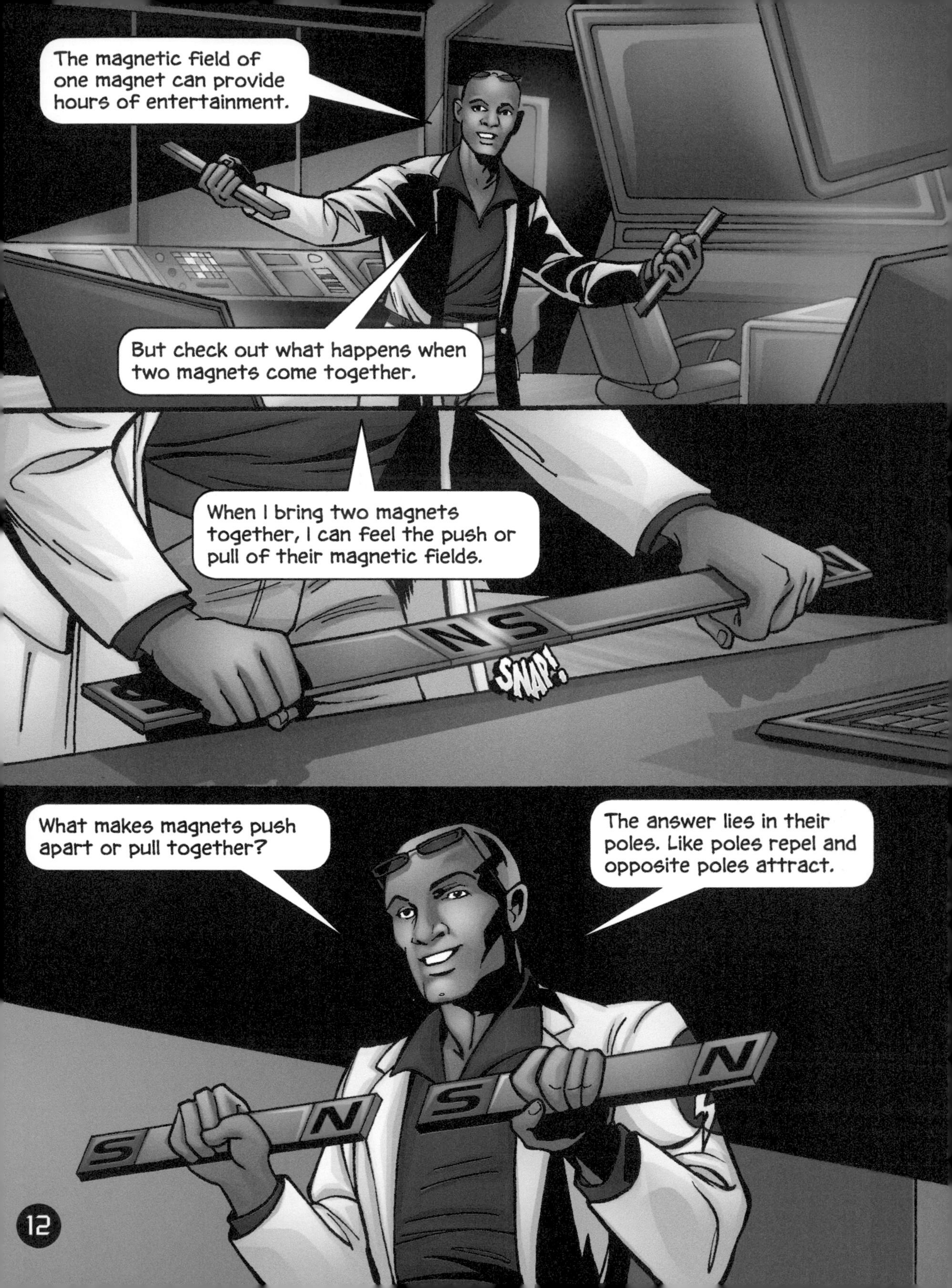
The magnetic field of one magnet can provide hours of entertainment.
But check out what happens when two magnets come together.
When I bring two magnets together, I can feel the push or pull of their magnetic fields.
N S
SNAP!
What makes magnets push apart or pull together?
The answer lies in their poles. Like poles repel and opposite poles attract.
S N S N

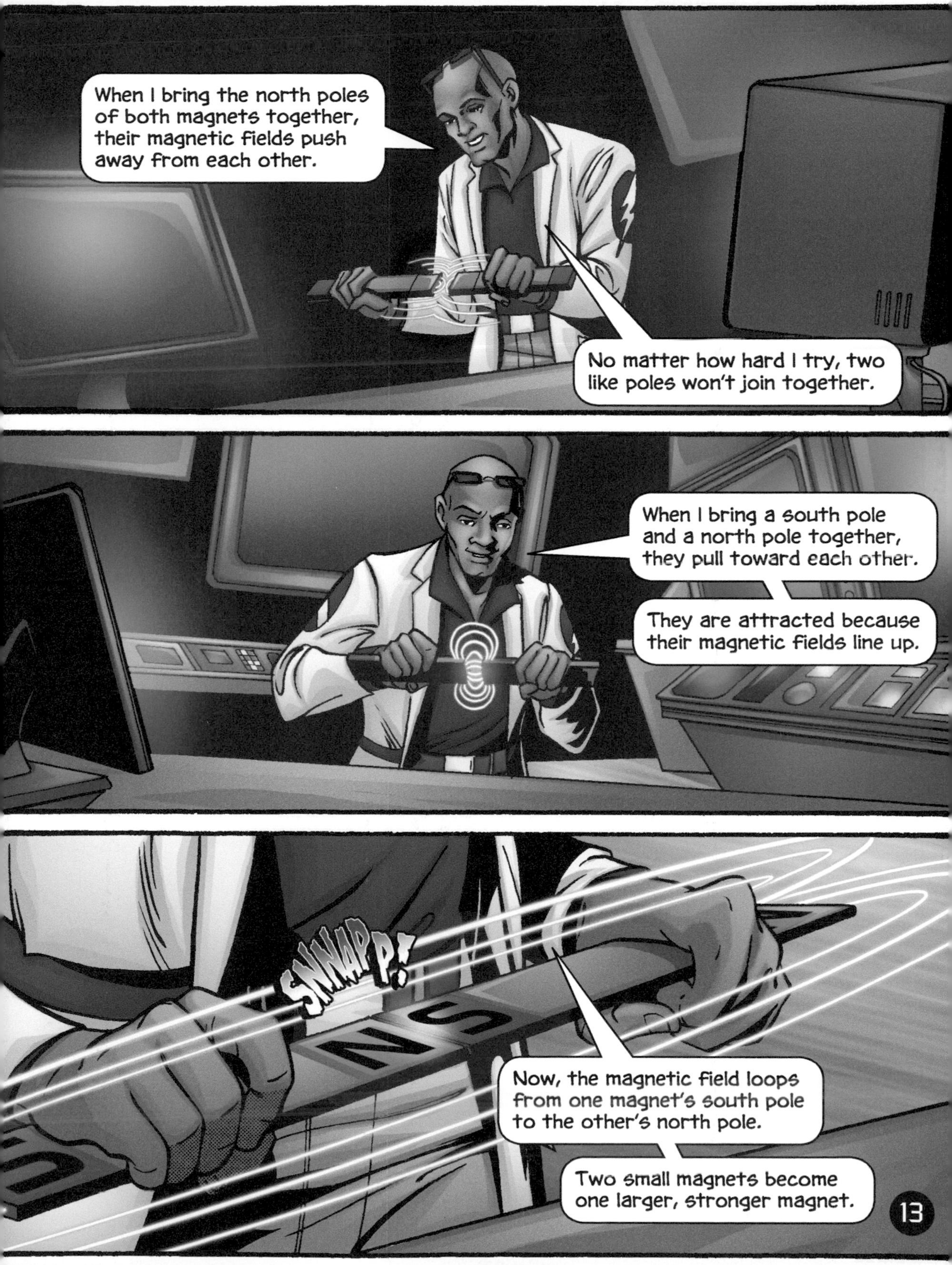
When I bring the north poles of both magnets together, their magnetic fields push away from each other.
No matter how hard I try, two like poles won't join together.
When I bring a south pole and a north pole together, they pull toward each other.
They are attracted because their magnetic fields line up.
SNNAPP!
N
S
Now, the magnetic field loops from one magnet's south pole to the other's north pole.
Two small magnets become one larger, stronger magnet.

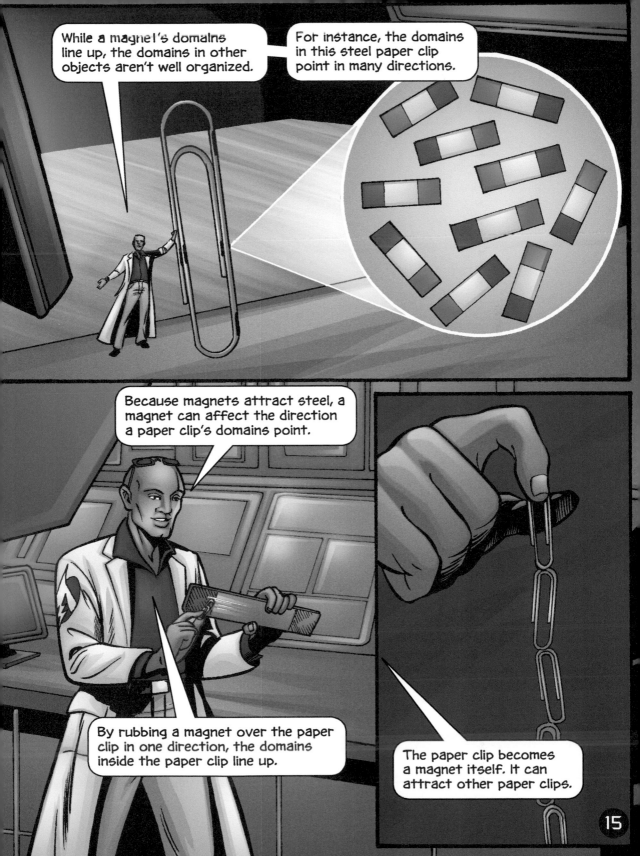

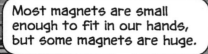

Most magnets are small enough to fit in our hands, but some magnets are huge.

I know a scientist in the Canadian Arctic who can tell us how our own planet acts like a giant magnet.

Hello, Max. What science topic are you studying this time?

Magnets, Dr. Mink. I need information about Earth's magnetic power.

Earth's magnetism comes from deep beneath its surface. In the planet's outer core, hot magma made of iron and nickel slowly rises and falls.

OUTER CORE

The moving magma creates electrical currents that form a magnetic field.

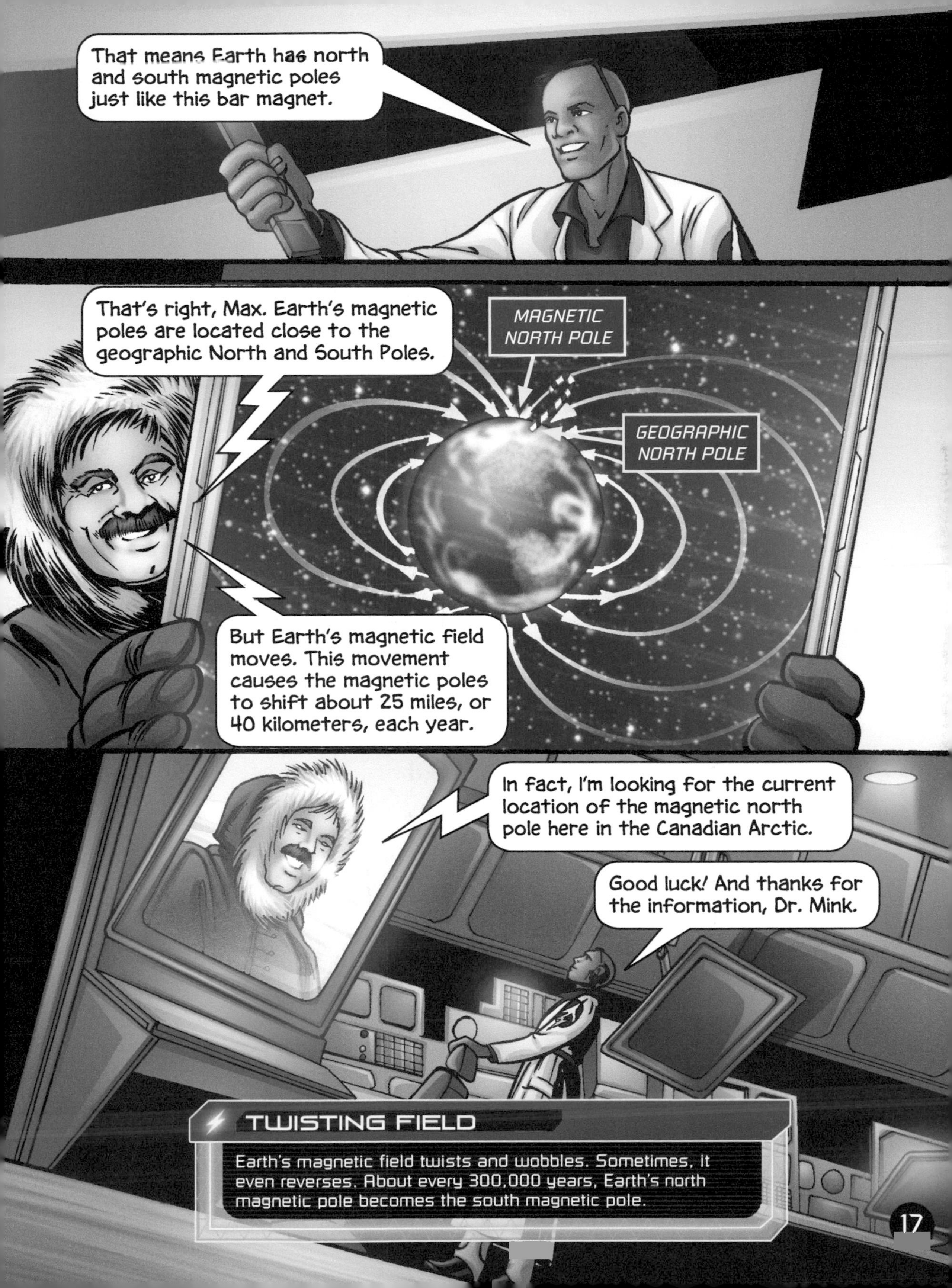
That means Earth has north and south magnetic poles just like this bar magnet.
That's right, Max. Earth's magnetic poles are located close to the geographic North and South Poles.
MAGNETIC NORTH POLE
GEOGRAPHIC NORTH POLE
But Earth's magnetic field moves. This movement causes the magnetic poles to shift about 25 miles, or 40 kilometers, each year.
In fact, I'm looking for the current location of the magnetic north pole here in the Canadian Arctic.
Good luck! And thanks for the information, Dr. Mink.

TWISTING FIELD

Earth's magnetic field twists and wobbles. Sometimes, it even reverses. About every 300,000 years, Earth's north magnetic pole becomes the south magnetic pole.

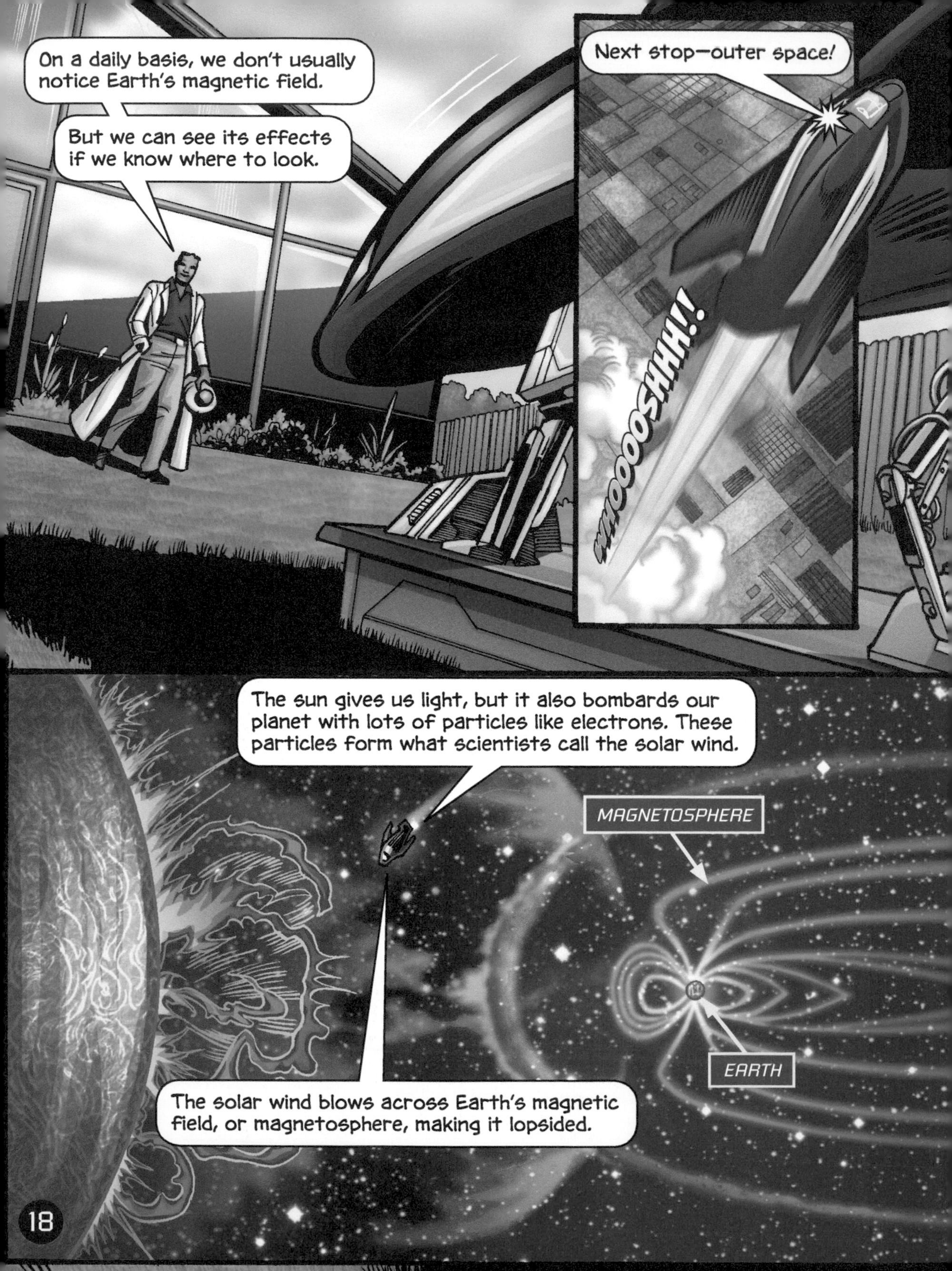
On a daily basis, we don't usually notice Earth's magnetic field.
But we can see its effects if we know where to look.
Next stop—outer space!
WHOOOOOSHHH!!
The sun gives us light, but it also bombards our planet with lots of particles like electrons. These particles form what scientists call the solar wind.
MAGNETOSPHERE
EARTH
The solar wind blows across Earth's magnetic field, or magnetosphere, making it lopsided.

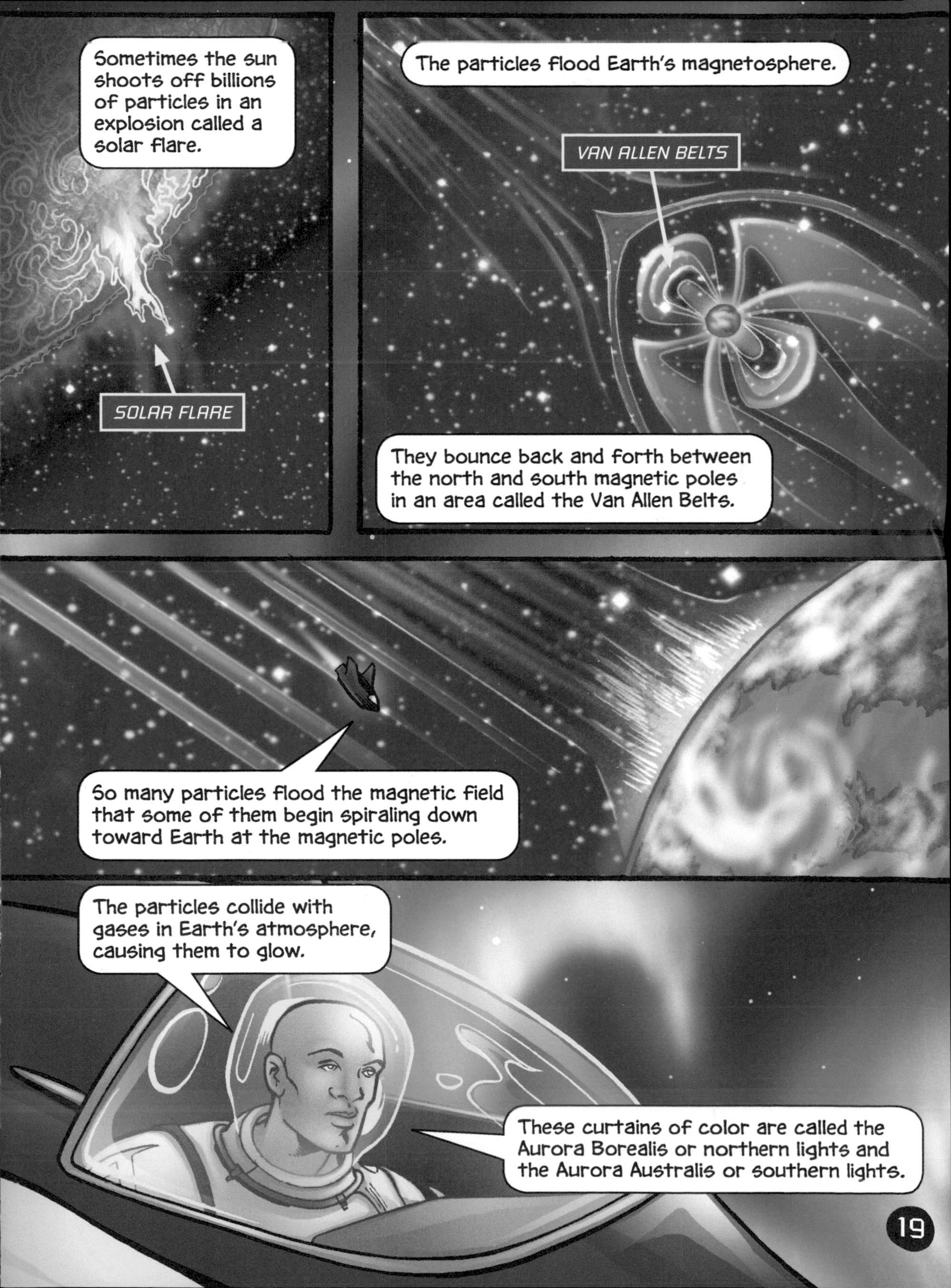
Sometimes the sun shoots off billions of particles in an explosion called a solar flare.
SOLAR FLARE
The particles flood Earth's magnetosphere.
VAN ALLEN BELTS
They bounce back and forth between the north and south magnetic poles in an area called the Van Allen Belts.
So many particles flood the magnetic field that some of them begin spiraling down toward Earth at the magnetic poles.
The particles collide with gases in Earth's atmosphere, causing them to glow.
These curtains of color are called the Aurora Borealis or northern lights and the Aurora Australis or southern lights.

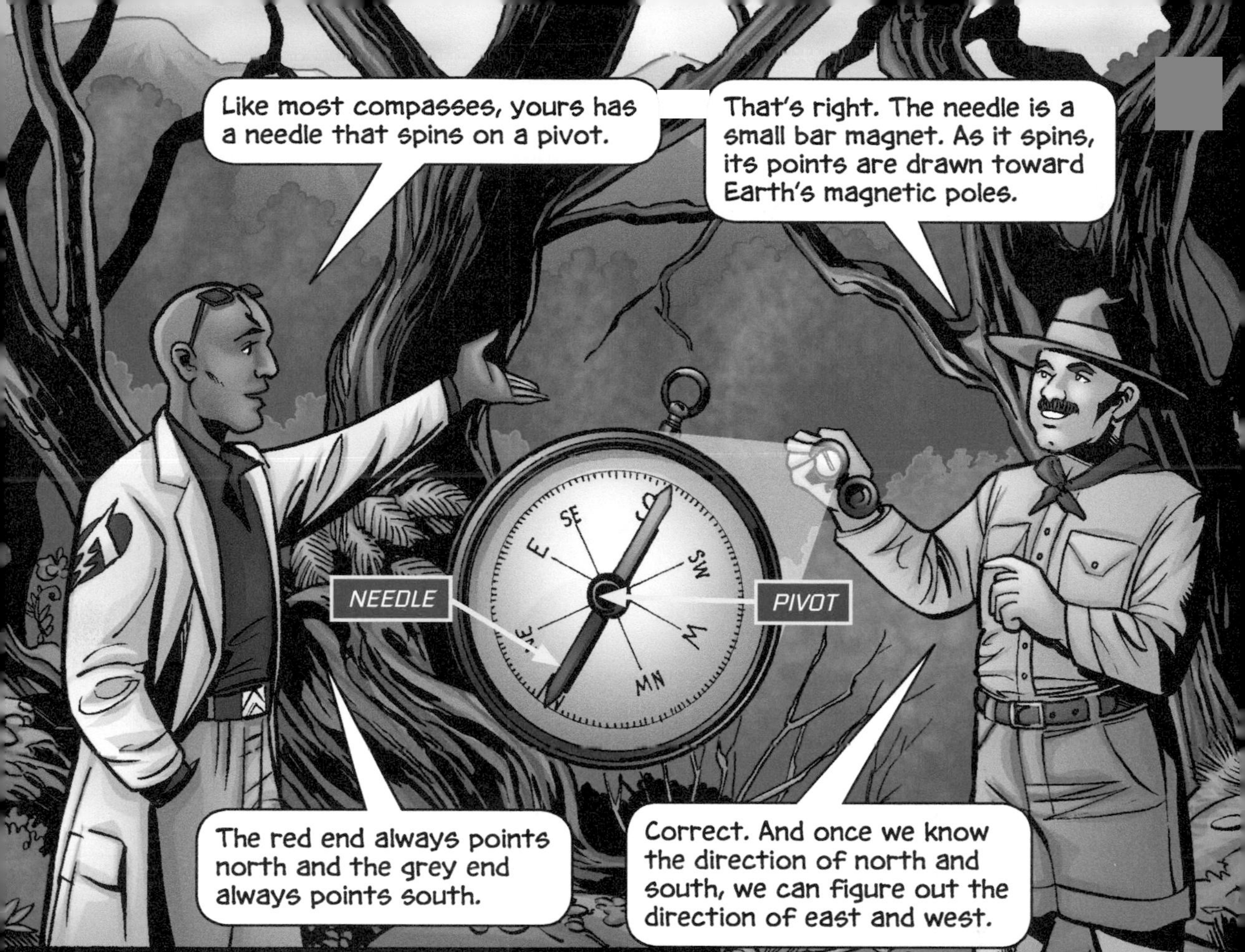
Like most compasses, yours has a needle that spins on a pivot.
That's right. The needle is a small bar magnet. As it spins, its points are drawn toward Earth's magnetic poles.
NEEDLE
PIVOT
The red end always points north and the grey end always points south.
Correct. And once we know the direction of north and south, we can figure out the direction of east and west.

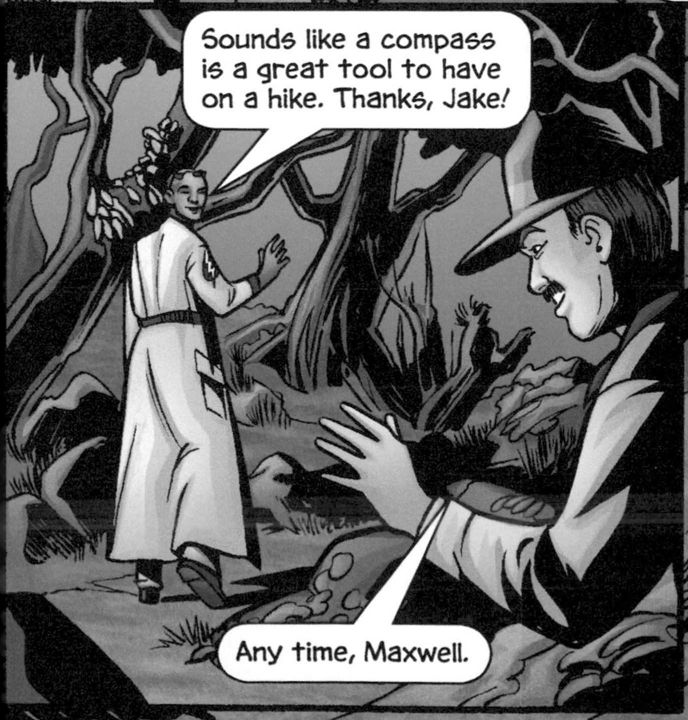
Sounds like a compass is a great tool to have on a hike. Thanks, Jake!
Any time, Maxwell.

FINDING EAST

Finding north and south on a compass is easy. But what about east or west? Finding these directions is easier than you think. To find east, hold the compass level and rotate it so the letter E is on top. Now, slowly turn your body until the red tip of the needle points to the letter N. When it does, you are facing east.

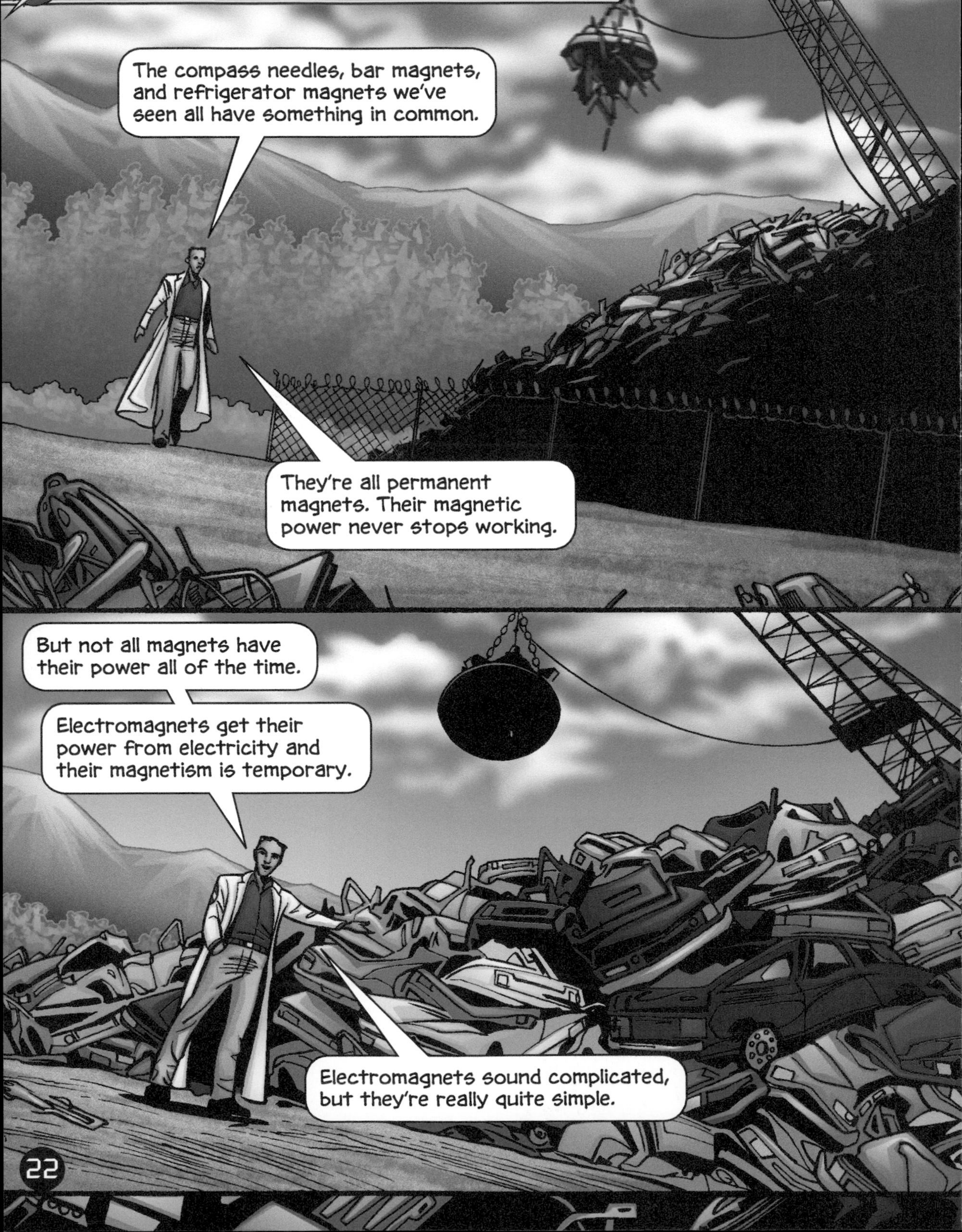
The compass needles, bar magnets, and refrigerator magnets we've seen all have something in common.
They're all permanent magnets. Their magnetic power never stops working.
But not all magnets have their power all of the time.
Electromagnets get their power from electricity and their magnetism is temporary.
Electromagnets sound complicated, but they're really quite simple.

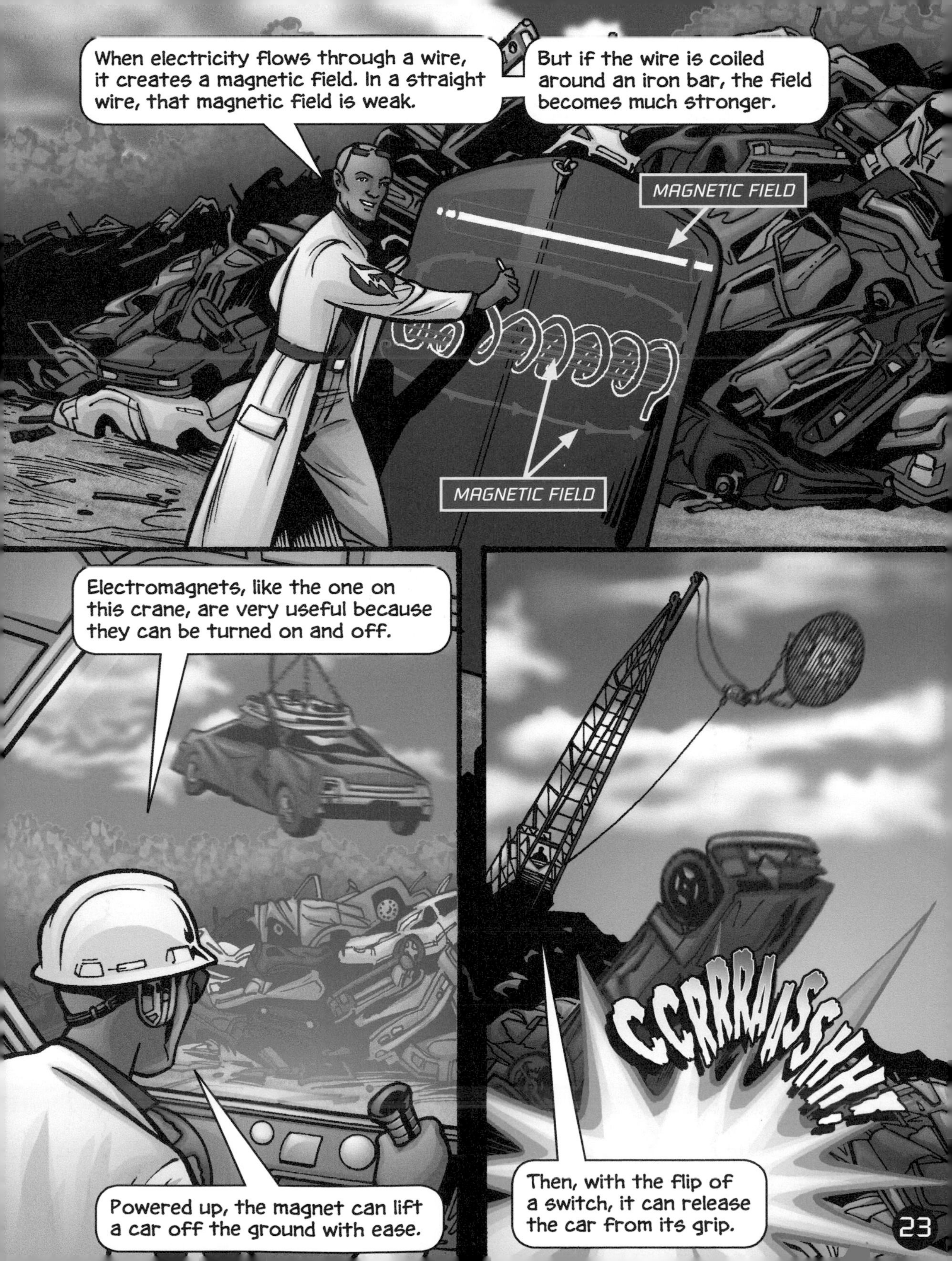
When electricity flows through a wire, it creates a magnetic field. In a straight wire, that magnetic field is weak.
But if the wire is coiled around an iron bar, the field becomes much stronger.
MAGNETIC FIELD
MAGNETIC FIELD
Electromagnets, like the one on this crane, are very useful because they can be turned on and off.
Powered up, the magnet can lift a car off the ground with ease.
CCRRRAASSHH!
Then, with the flip of a switch, it can release the car from its grip.

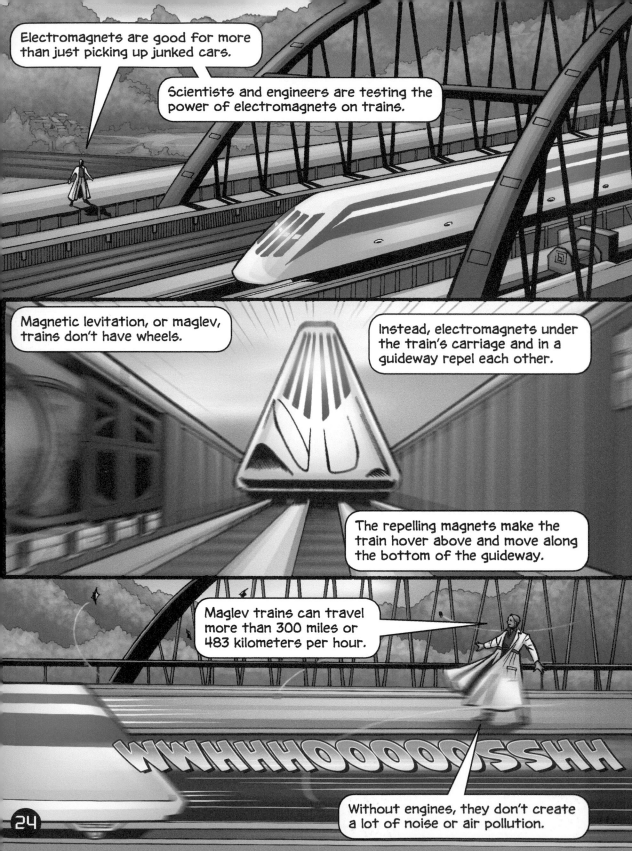

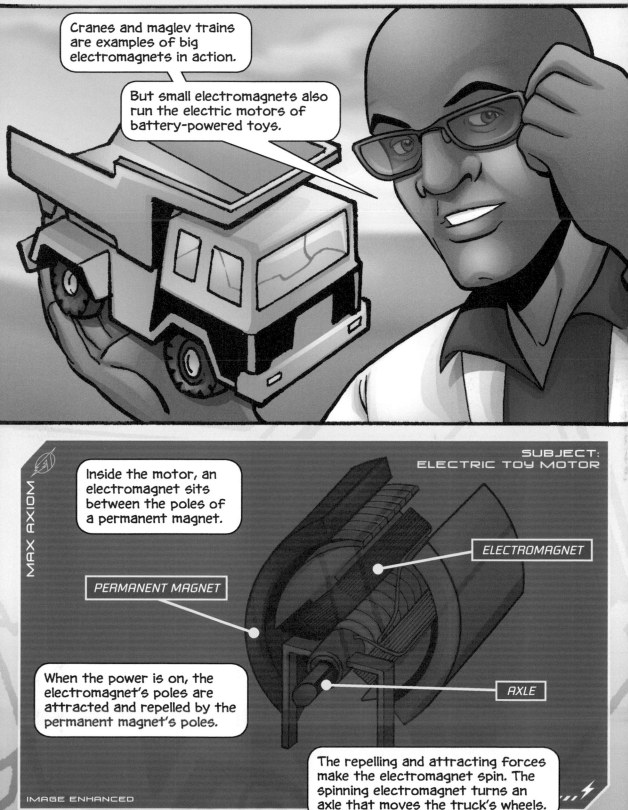

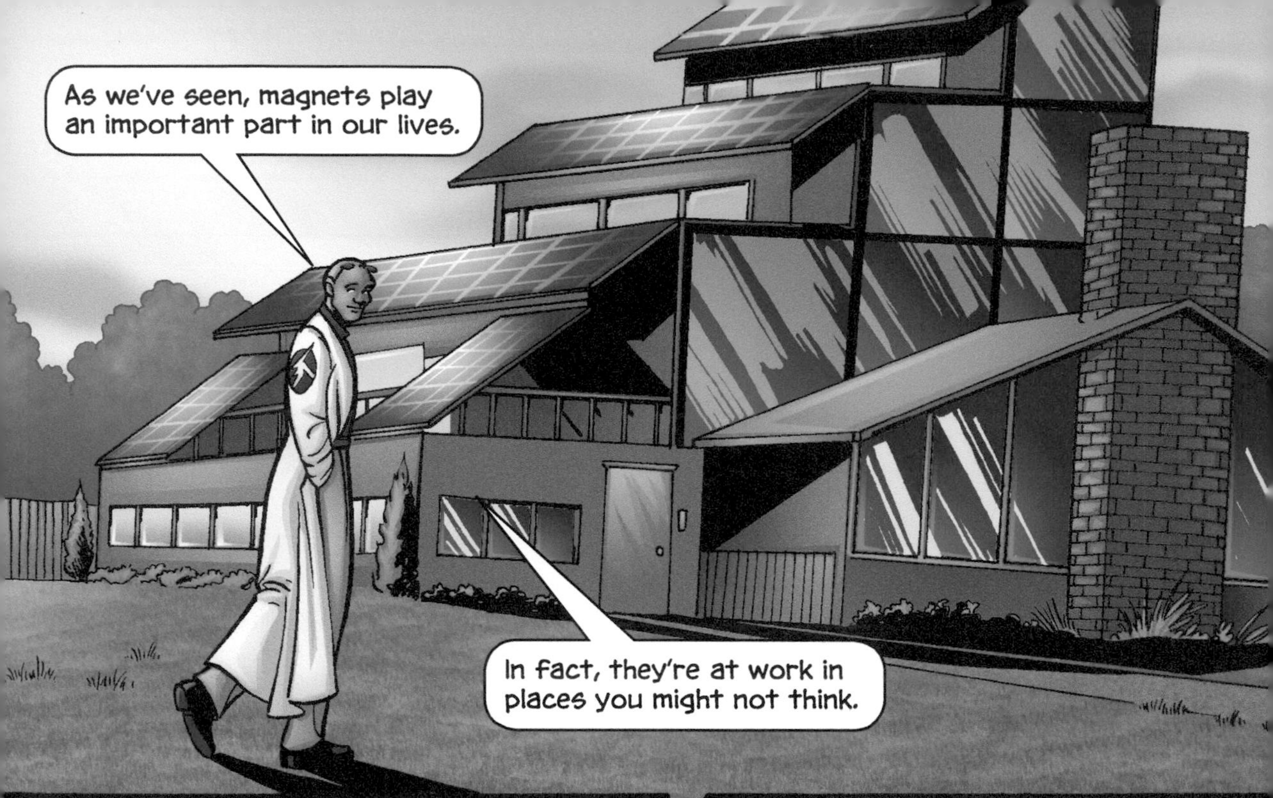
As we've seen, magnets play an important part in our lives.
In fact, they're at work in places you might not think.

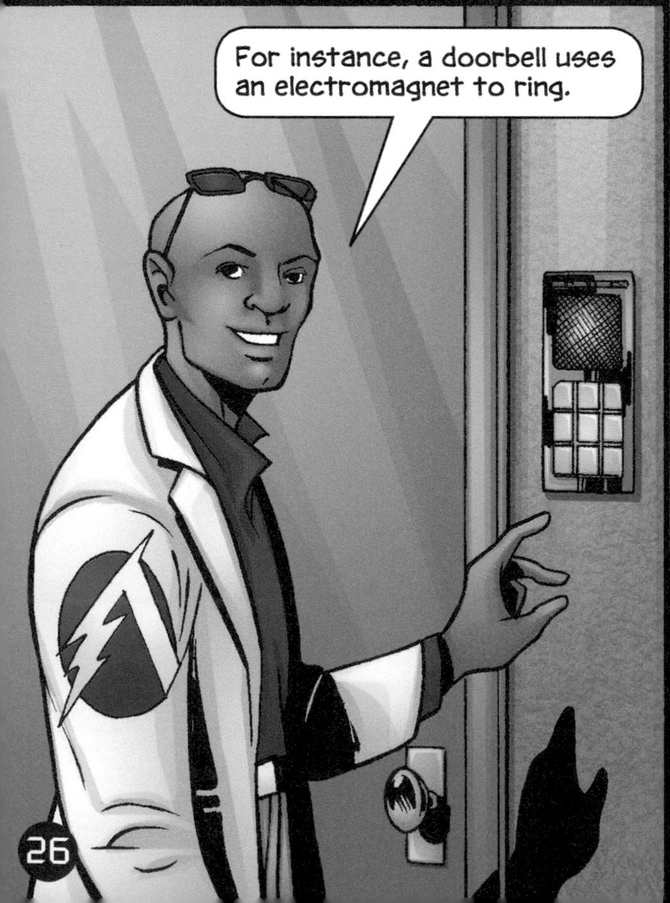
For instance, a doorbell uses an electromagnet to ring.

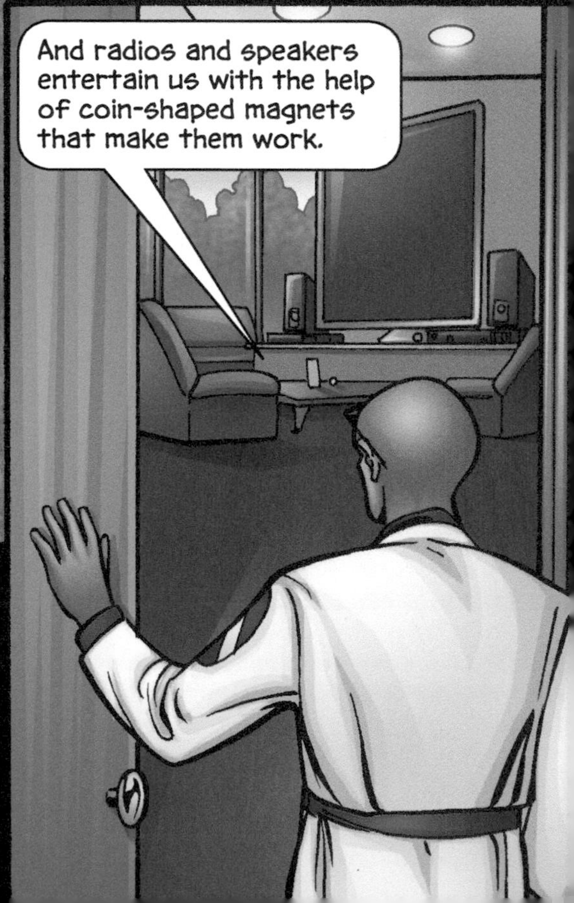
And radios and speakers entertain us with the help of coin-shaped magnets that make them work.

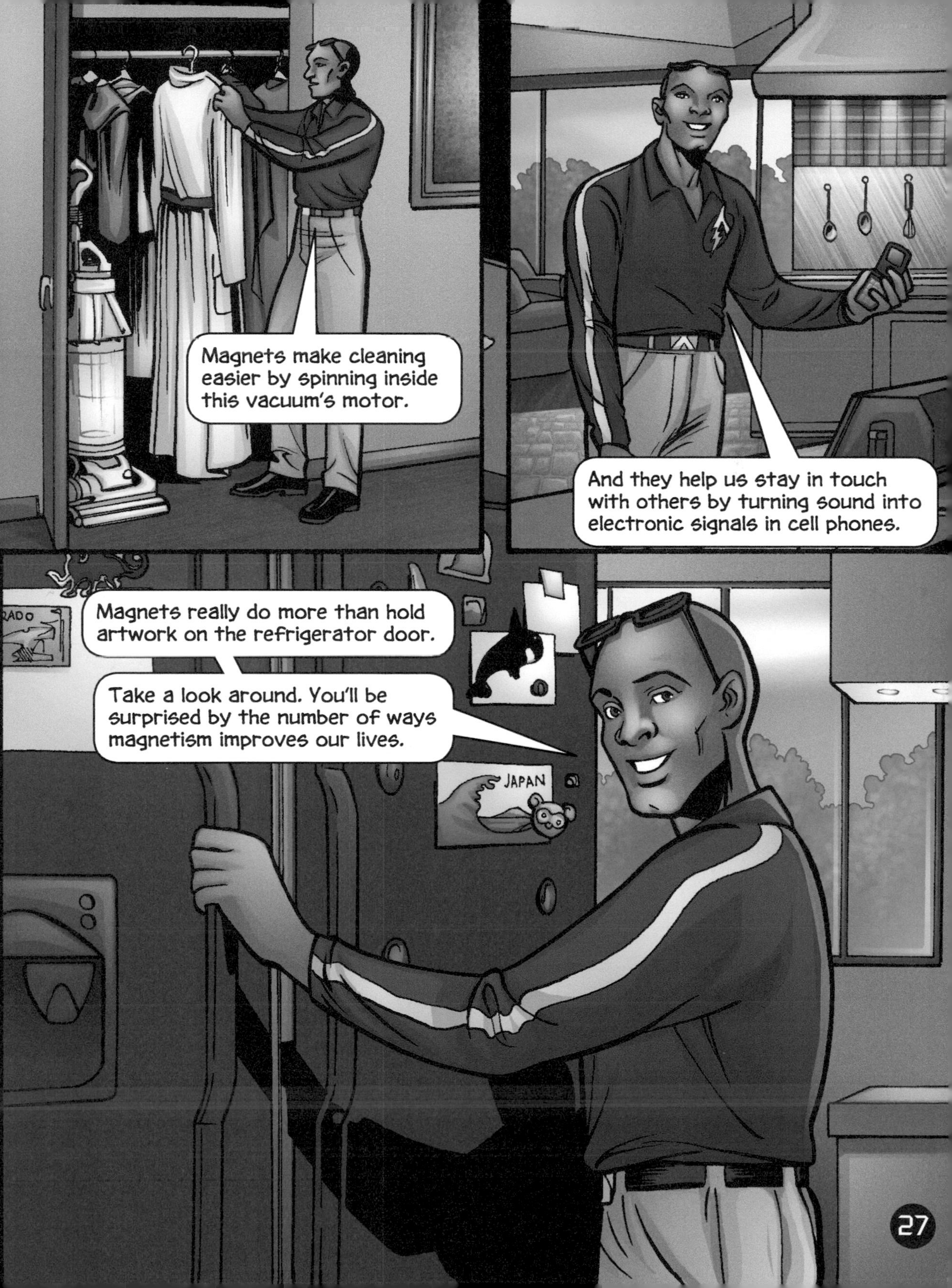

Magnets make cleaning easier by spinning inside this vacuum's motor.
And they help us stay in touch with others by turning sound into electronic signals in cell phones.
Magnets really do more than hold artwork on the refrigerator door.
Take a look around. You'll be surprised by the number of ways magnetism improves our lives.
JAPAN

MORE ABOUT MAGNETISM

Some animals sense Earth's magnetic field and use it to help them find their way. Whales, dolphins, and many birds use Earth's magnetic field during migration. Australia's compass termites always build their nests facing north.

Earth's north magnetic pole has moved about 700 miles (1,127 kilometers) since it was first discovered in 1831. If it continues moving at its current speed and direction, the north magnetic pole will be located in Siberia by 2050.

Some farmers make their cattle swallow a magnet to keep them healthy. This small magnet attracts nails and pieces of wire they accidentally eat while grazing. The magnet keeps the bits of metal from passing through their stomachs and damaging their other organs.

The National High Magnetic Field Laboratory at Florida State University in Tallahassee has the world's largest magnet. This giant magnet stands 16 feet (5 meters) tall and weighs more than 30,000 pounds (13,608 kilograms). Scientists developed the magnet for 13 years at a cost of $16.5 million.

The sun has a very strong magnetic field. Over time, this field gets knotted and twisted creating dark-colored sunspots on the sun's surface. Sunspots always come in pairs. One is a north magnetic pole while the other is a south magnetic pole.

The sun's magnetic field flips every 11 years. The north magnetic pole becomes a south magnetic pole and the south magnetic pole becomes a north magnetic pole.

Can a magnet attract a penny? Not a United States penny. U.S. pennies are made mostly of zinc and copper. Neither zinc nor copper is magnetic. British pennies are another story. They are made mostly of steel coated with a thin layer of copper. A magnet will easily pick up British pennies because magnets attract steel.

MAKING MAGNETS

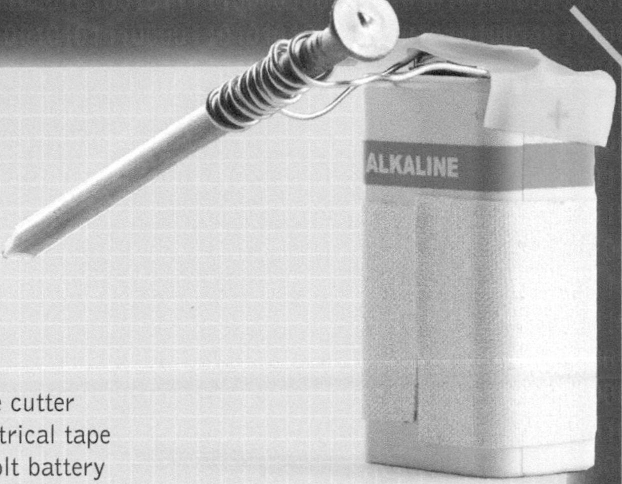
ALKALINE

Attract a reputation as a magnetism expert by crafting your very own electromagnet that really works!

WHAT YOU NEED:

- large steel nail
- paper clips
- paper and pencil
- strong bar magnet
- copper wire
- wire cutter
- electrical tape
- 9-volt battery
- staples

WHAT YOU DO:

Part I

1. Place the steel nail next to a paper clip. What happens? Write down what you observe on a piece of paper.
2. Rub the bar magnet against the nail, from one end to the other, in one direction. Repeat 10 times. Each time, lift the magnet off the nail before returning it to its starting position.
3. Place the nail next to the paper clip again. What do you notice? Write down your observations.

Part II

1. Use a wire cutter to cut an 10-inch (25-centimeter) piece of copper wire.
2. Leave about 3 inches (7.5 centimeters) loose, then coil the wire around the nail until you reach the nail's tip, leaving another 3 inches (7.5 centimeters) loose on this end.
3. Tape the ends of the wire to the connectors on the top of the battery, one end on each connector. Be careful, the wire may get hot once connected.
4. The coiled nail is now an electromagnet! Experiment with its ability to move or pick up paper clips or staples.
5. Take apart your electromagnet when you are finished.

DISCUSSION QUESTIONS

1. Magnets can hold papers to refrigerators. What are three other things you use magnets for every single day? Which one would be the hardest for you to live without?

2. Auroras are seen only near the North Pole and the South Pole. Why are they only visible there?

3. Earth has its own magnetic field. What are the factors that cause it, and how does it change in different locations?

4. Rubbing a magnet on a paper clip makes the paper clip magnetic. How does this process work?

WRITING PROMPTS

1. What is a magnetic field? Write down a definition in your own words based on what you've read in the book.

2. More iron filings stick to the ends of a magnet than stick to the middle of the magnet. Write a short paragraph explaining why this is the case, and draw a picture of what this magnetic process looks like.

3. A compass is a useful magnetic tool for finding a direction. Write a short story in which you use a compass to find your way in the wilderness.

4. An important part of an electromagnet is the wire coiled around an iron bar. Write a paragraph explaining how an electromagnet works and why the coils of wire are so important.

TAKE A QUIZ!

GLOSSARY

atom (AT-uhm)—an element in its smallest form

domain (doh-MAYN)—a group of magnetic atoms

electromagnet (e-lek-troh-MAG-nit)—a temporary magnet created when an electric current flows through a conductor

electron (e-LEK-tron)—a tiny particle in an atom that travels around the nucleus

magma (MAG-muh)—melted rock found beneath the surface of Earth

magnetic field (mag-NET-ik FEELD)—the area around a magnet that has the power to attract magnetic metals

magnetite (MAG-nuh-tite)—a hard, black rock found in Earth that attracts iron; magnetite is also known as lodestone

magnetosphere (mag-NET-ohs-sfir)—the magnetic field extending into space around a planet or star

nucleus (NOO-klee-uhss)—the center of an atom; a nucleus is made up of neutrons and protons

pivot (PIV-uht)—a point on which something turns or balances

pole (POHL)—one of the two ends of a magnet; a pole can also be the top or bottom part of a planet.

repel (ri-PEL)—to push apart; like poles of magnets repel each other

temporary (TEM-puh-rer-ee)—lasting only a short time

READ MORE

Arbuthnott, Gill. *Your Guide to Electricity and Magnetism*. Drawn to Science: Illustrated Guides to Key Science Concepts. New York: Crabtree Publishing Company, 2018.

Canavan, Thomas. *Excellent Experiments with Electricity and Magnetism*. Mind-Blowing Science Experiments. New York: Gareth Stevens Publishing, 2017.

Forest, Christopher. *Focus on Magnetism*. Hands-On STEM. Mendota Heights, Minn.: North Star Editions, 2017.

Spilsbury, Richard. *Investigating Magnetism*. Investigating Science Challenges. New York: Crabtree Publishing Company, 2018.

INTERNET SITES

Use Facthound to find Internet sites related to this book.

Visit *www.facthound.com*

Just type in 9781543529500 and go!

 Check out projects, games and lots more at
www.capstonekids.com

INDEX